BLUEPRINT FOR PROGRESS

Al-Anon's Fourth Step Inventory

The Al-Anon Family Groups are a fellowship of relatives and friends of alcoholics who share their experience, strength, and hope in order to solve their common problems. We believe alcoholism is a family illness and that changed attitudes can aid recovery.

Al-Anon is not allied with any sect, denomination, political entity, organization, or institution; does not engage in any controversy; neither endorses nor opposes any cause. There are no dues for membership. Al-Anon is self-supporting through its own voluntary contributions.

Al-Anon has but one purpose: to help families of alcoholics. We do this by practicing the Twelve Steps, by welcoming and giving comfort to families of alcoholics, and by giving understanding and encouragement to the alcoholic.

Suggested Al-Anon Preamble to the Twelve Steps

For information and catalog of literature write:
Al-Anon Family Group Headquarters, Inc.
1600 Corporate Landing Parkway, Virginia Beach, VA 23454-5617
Phone: (757) 563-1600 Fax: (757) 563-1656
al-anon.org wso@al-anon.org

Al-Anon/Alateen is supported by members' voluntary contributions and from the sale of our Confer-ence Approved Literature.

ISBN- 0-910034-42-7

Approved by
World Service Conference
Al-Anon Family Groups

21-5 P-91 Printed in U.S.A.

TABLE OF CONTENTS

SERENITY PRAYER

God grant me the serenity
To accept the things I cannot change,
Courage to change the things I can,
And wisdom to know the difference.

STEP FOUR

Made a searching and fearless moral inventory of ourselves.

THE PURPOSE OF STEP FOUR

The Fourth Step can be an essential tool for personal growth. Many of us have been so obsessed with the behavior of an alcoholic that we developed a limited sense of ourselves. We may have lost sight of our personal goals, neglected our potential, and become too concerned with our attempts to change someone else. Often our good qualities lay hidden behind frustration and fear.

Thanks to our work with the first three Steps, we are preparing to summon the courage to look at who we really are. After we admitted our powerlessness over alcohol and its effects on our lives, we received encouragement to let go and to stop managing the affairs of others. Admitting that our own lives had become unmanageable suggests we could use some help.

The Second Step introduced us to the idea of a Power greater than ourselves, a source where we could find that help. Soon we learned to trust that Higher Power to restore our emotional and spiritual balance, so we can begin to realize our full potential.

Step Three prepared us to take action. We made the decision to place our will and our lives into the care of our Higher Power. Doing this, most of us felt assurance that we were cared for and loved. We received specific encouragement to live as our Higher Power wants us to live, rather than the painful way that we had lived for so long.

Some members summarize the first three Steps by saying, "I can't. God can. I think I'll let Him." Ironically enough, the same thinking prevails if we apply this wisdom in dealing with our alcoholic loved one.

This brings us to the Fourth Step where the task is to make a "searching and fearless moral inventory of ourselves." We can do this by answering questions about some of our personal habits, actions, and reactions. Our goal is to learn as much as we can about ourselves, both the good and the not-so-good.

Step Four is an exercise in perception, a way to distinguish between what works in our lives and what is no longer useful or necessary. Being aware of what we did yesterday can help us understand and accept who we are today, so tomorrow we can become the people we want to be. It is not the purpose of the Fourth Step to degrade ourselves, but to find out the types of mistakes that we tend to make. Initially our only task is to be as honest as we can.

The experience of countless Al-Anon members who have already worked this Step assures us that the process uncovered their good qualities too. We may find that some of our defects of character are actually assets gone astray. It might turn out that some of our faults are only shortcomings, areas where we have fallen short of our intentions, rather than personal failures or things that we decided to do wrong. If we are truly honest, we will find out certain things that we did wrong, and identify some of the people to whom we owe amends.

An inventory is a practical thing—a list of stock on hand. It requires seriousness, time, and effort. To get a total and accurate picture, we take a written inventory to see where the business of living is going well and where it is not. An inventory is a method of gathering information. For many of us, the more information we learn about ourselves in a broad range of categories, the better we can understand who we are and how we got this way. In order to measure personal progress, it has proven advantageous to date our answers. This will provide a clear point of reference for the future and a way to compare the results over a period of time.

There is no perfect way to do Step Four, but it is important simply to tell it like it is and to identify the areas where we have experienced the most trouble. It is also important to explore those areas where we have shown our greatest strengths. Our experience shows us that working with a knowledgeable Sponsor can help put us at ease and ensure that we get the full benefit of the healing process.

We can choose to work by ourselves, writing our answers to the questions in this workbook and noting our own observations about our progress. The process of putting thoughts on paper can stimulate vital insights about our recovery. Whether we choose to work by ourselves or with someone, it is worth remembering that in Al-Anon we never have to do anything alone. Our Higher Power is always with us.

The format of this workbook might provide handy ideas for leading a meeting or a series of meetings on Step Four. Listening as trusted friends share their personal experience can remind us that our willingness to seek improvement is one of our greatest assets.

Most sections of this workbook also include reflections from fellow members who willingly share experience, strength, and hope with us through an array of Conference Approved Literature. The workbook questions and exercises are solely designed to help us learn about ourselves. While there are no right or wrong answers, some subjects may challenge us more than others to be truly honest with ourselves.

Remember, in Step Three we already "Made a decision to turn our will and our lives over to the care of God *as we understood Him.*"

Reflections

"With or without fear, as I sought out my hidden beliefs and brought them into the light, I found that sometimes I was wrong—but not always. Sometimes I knew truths about myself but I lacked the confidence to stand by them." (*Paths to Recovery*, p. 47)

HONESTY

Chaos, uncertainty, and confusion can make it difficult to see the truth. Because reality is sometimes painful, facts get distorted and fantasy offers a way to cope. Without realizing it, bad situations become temporary speed bumps. We may have told ourselves that the alcoholic was not hung-over; he or she was just having a bad day. The checking account was not really overdrawn; there was a bank error. We were not rude to our neighbors; they were simply overreacting. Eventually such lies insured peace in the home, and after all our only goal was temporary sanity.

Step Four asks that we be honest with ourselves about ourselves. Our part, our response to the disease of alcoholism, and the decisions we made in this merry-go-round environment, are the only things for which we are responsible. Here we face the reality of our circumstances so we can accept our lives for what they are, based upon the facts. Our purpose is to see who we are, how we got that way, and the characteristics that are ours to work with. In this way we take a positive step toward recovery.

Reflections

"It would have been easier to simply continue feeling frustrated and resentful over my disappointment with the alcoholic, but it wouldn't have helped me to live a happier or more satisfying life. Although it was hard and sometimes embarrassing work, the self-honesty I learned in Al-Anon helped me to create a far better life than the one I'd been living." (*How Al-Anon Works*, p. 172)

Questions

1. Dishonesty as a Part of Our Lives

How did I fail to tell the truth as a child?

To whom did I lie?

What were some of the results of my misrepresentations?

Whom have I hurt by being dishonest?

2. Dishonesty as Adults

What did I bring home from work or school that wasn't mine?

Have I ever stolen anything while I was shopping?

If I cheated on games or examinations, which ones were they?

Have I misrepresented expense sheets or personal income taxes?

In what relationships have I ever been unfaithful?

What traffic laws do I know I have violated?

When did I ask others to lie for me?

What do I do when other people ask me to lie or cheat for them?

3. Dishonest/Honest Habits

What specific deceptions do I commit for other people?

How do I react when someone draws untrue conclusions about people, places, or things?

When did my silence help support someone else's lie?

What stories about others do I pass on without checking to see if they are true?

How do I compliment people when I feel they have done a good job?

How can I tell the difference between the way things look to me and the way they really are?

How do I usually react when I find out someone has misrepresented something to me?

In my interactions with others, do I tell the truth or do I say what they want to hear most of the time? Under what circumstances?

How can my Higher Power help me to tell the truth?

Findings

By answering these questions on the subject of honesty, what have I learned about myself?

SELF-WORTH

With some of us, the awareness of our importance and value as human beings was nourished from the beginning. For many of us, however, living within the grasp of the disease of alcoholism seriously affec-ted our outlook. We hid our feelings of self-worth deep within, and our perspective became distorted. Many of us even tried to conceal that we felt worthless on the inside to the point that we couldn't show any real warmth and concern for anyone, including ourselves. A little work in the right direction can revive our natural gifts that have been hidden by years of dysfunction.

If we feel guilty because we think we caused the problem, if we doubt our ability to do anything right, or if our fear of change has turned into a real sense of self-hatred, then it is to our advantage to tap into our abilities of patience, honesty, and willingness. We do this to get on the road to recovery.

The Fourth Step offers a new beginning by showing us that we are worthwhile people even though we have made mistakes. Eventually we learn to accept ourselves as we are, to respect ourselves for what we have lived through, and even to appreciate some of the good qualities that are important parts of our personalities. Finding our true self-worth is a process of self-examination.

Reflections

Because I didn't have a good opinion of myself, I was concerned with what others thought of me, and any kind of disapproval or rejection made me uncomfortable. If others liked me, then I felt good about myself. If they disliked me, or criticized me, I felt compelled to change to please them. My opinion of myself depended entirely on others. Today I realize that, instead of putting the opinions of others first, I must work on improving my own feelings of self-worth. As long as I feel like a truly worthwhile person, I can be less concerned with what others think.

Questions

1. Treating Ourselves Well

What do I do to take care of myself physically?

What is my plan for eating the right foods and for getting enough rest?

When was the last time I went to the doctor and dentist for my own checkup?

What are my reasons for wearing or not wearing a seatbelt in a car?

What am I doing to exercise my mind so that I can learn new things?

What do I usually do when someone pays me a compliment?

How comfortable am I in my relationship with my Higher Power?

2. Safety First

How can I prevent others from abusing me physically, mentally, or emotionally?

How do I know when another's behavior is unacceptable to me?

How do I feel about myself when I am in an abusive situation?

What am I doing to protect myself from abuse?

How do I let another know that his or her behavior is unacceptable to me?

3. Being Loveable

What do I like about myself?

What do other people like about me?

Can I derive satisfaction out of working to improve myself? Explain.

4. My Own Standards

What are my spiritual needs?

What are my limitations and do I accept them?

How can I learn to sit quietly in the middle of an outburst and remember that the accusations made against me may not be the facts?

What were the times in my life when I experienced the most self-confidence?

What are some of the things I know how to do that make me feel especially proud of myself?

5. Checking Myself

Whom do I rely on to fulfill my emotional needs, and how is that working?

What stops me from doing what I really like to do?

How do I react or respond when someone offers to help me do something?

What about my education do I wish was different and why?

How much time do I spend alone, and what are some of the things I do when I am by myself?

What do I like and not like about my physical appearance?

How does my current attitude toward my self-worth affect my family?

Findings

By answering these questions on the subject of self-worth, what have I learned about myself?

FEAR

Many of us who have lived with alcoholism became intimately acquainted with fear. We feared the alcoholics might harm us or someone else, or that they might hurt themselves. We feared the bills would not be paid, or we worried about who knew the truth of our situation. Some of us felt afraid to live our own lives. We were dying on the inside as we constantly said, "What if . . .?" The energy it took for us to lead double lives was exhausting.

In Al-Anon we began to learn that fear is nothing more than a lack of faith, and that by developing our faith we can have courage beyond our expectations. Eventually we looked at our problems and ourselves differently.

Some of the choices that help us today become clearer in the Fourth Step inventory process. We begin to understand what we did, and that leads to compassion for who we used to be. Our growing awareness about the truth of our situation points us toward freedom. As we face reality, we begin to move forward with a new confidence.

The Al-Anon recovery program does not guarantee we will feel no fear. It shows us we can acknowledge our fear and remain free to live life anyway, under the care of our Higher Power.

Reflections

"Fear dominated my life. Denial clouded my perception. I ignored reality because it hurt when I thought about it. When painful thoughts emerged, as they inevitably did, I quickly and anxiously shoved them away. It was as if my thoughts were my enemies, and as they approached, I turned and ran as fast as possible in the opposite direction. Instead of expending my energy on living my life, I focused almost exclusively on avoiding pain, stuffing disturbing feelings, and keeping myself as numb as I could." (*How Al-Anon Works*, p. 154)

Questions

1. Facing Our Fears

How do I usually react when I feel frightened?

What provokes my fears?

What fears do I have about the alcoholics in my life?

Where do I turn when I feel afraid, and does that relieve my fear?

How do I interact with authority figures?

2. The Results of My Fears

If my worst fears came true, how would they impact me?

What happened the last time I was truly afraid and how did I respond?

How do my fears affect the way I make decisions?

3. Coping with My Fears

What am I afraid of today?

How do my fears of the alcoholic affect the way I interact with him/her?

How do I include my Higher Power when I feel afraid, and what is the result?

In what ways do I have any fear of my Higher Power?

Findings

By answering these questions on the subject of fear, what have I learned about myself?

ANGER

Alcoholism left many of us with a great deal of anger. Broken dreams, ruined finances, and loss of trust generated strong desires to blame someone. In frustration we watched and tried to ignore the turmoil swirling around us as our loved one struggled with alcoholism. At times we even felt that any kind of anger was wrong and we denied that it controlled many of our reactions. We felt uneasy when others expressed their anger openly.

If we examine the times when we became angry, what we felt angry about, and who was present when our anger began, we might be able to realize safe ways of expressing our feelings. By accepting that we sometimes have angry feelings and giving ourselves permission to feel them, we might free ourselves to feel all of our feelings—not just the angry ones.

A searching personal inventory can help us recognize and understand our anger.

Reflections

"Have I ever sought to find the tiny spark that detonated a family row that brought into the open ugly words and violent recriminations? Can I admit that I may have caused it by being too quick to react to a ridiculous accusation or denunciation? Do I take everything the alcoholic says—in his frustrated rage against *himself*—as offense to me?" (*One Day at a Time*, p. 55)

Questions

1. Anger Around Me

When I was young, how did the adults in my family express their anger?

What did I do that provoked anger from adults?

How did I respond as a young person to anger directed toward me?

How did I express my anger?

As a young person, what happened when I expressed anger?

2. Managing My Anger

What are some of the reasons why I feel angry with myself?

What do I do when someone is angry with me?

How do I usually express my anger?

What are some of the consequences of my anger?

In what situations has my anger been appropriate?

3. Anger in Relationships

When I am angry with people, how do I usually treat them?

How do my actions differ, depending on the individual I'm angry with?

How much power do I give to people who are angry with me?

How much power do I think I have when I feel very angry?

How have I used my anger to help someone?

4. Controlling My Anger

What was the most recent situation in which I felt angry?

What circumstances provoke my anger today? Make a list.

Where does alcoholism rank on my anger list?

Who are the people I tend to feel angry with? Name them and explain.

How important is it for me to continue feeling angry with certain people?

Findings

By answering these questions on the subject of anger, what have I learned about myself?

RESENTMENT

Many of us became angry when the active alcoholic could not or would not take his or her responsibilities seriously. Life wasn't fair. Later the alcoholic may even have found sobriety while we continued to brood over events from the past. As the alcoholic learned how to work a successful program of recovery, we may have felt neglected and abandoned. First we felt we had lost our loved one to drink, and then we felt we lost him or her to recovery. These ongoing, ill feelings are known as resentments and they can hurt us beyond measure.

We might carry such ill feelings for extended periods of time—sometimes so long after the original event has passed that we don't remember what triggered them in the first place. Even worse, the people we resent are unaware that we are upset. They go on to live their lives as they choose, while we remain bogged down in bitterness and negative thinking. An Al-Anon member once described such resentment as "the poison I take hoping that you will die!"

But the things that originally hurt were real to us. Broken promises, embarrassment, financial problems, neglect, and even violent acts really happened. These are scars that many of us have in common because of alcoholism. That was then—this is now.

In looking for the antidote for such resentments, we ask for help from our Higher Power as we seek to understand our own actions and motives. We try to face up to the consequences of what we have done and to concentrate on our part, the part we can do something about. Eventually we find solutions that lead to serenity and peace.

Reflections

"In the past, in alcoholic situations, I had learned it was best to keep my mouth shut when I was hurt. In Al-Anon, I have learned that when I don't communicate, I often get resentful. I start to think I am owed amends. When I blame someone else for the way I feel, I am probably avoiding facing my own responsibilities." (. . . *In All Our Affairs*, p. 196)

Questions

1. Resentments from Long Ago

Are there any people or organizations from childhood that I still feel angry with today? If so, list them and explain.

With the people I resent the most, what part did I play in the original events that happened?

How did I feel about the way my family dealt with angry situations?

2. Current Resentments

Who are the people in my life that I resent the most?

What reasons do I give for remaining angry for a long time?

What bothered me about the people I resent most?

How do my resentments affect me?

How do I usually treat those I resent?

How do I react to other people's good fortune?

3. Personal Conduct

How do I feel and act when people in my life fail to meet my expectations?

How do I cope with rejection?

Do I resent it when I'm asked to do something that I don't want to do?

If I want to stop feeling the pain from my own resentments, whom do I need to forgive?

Findings

By answering these questions on the subject of resentment, what have I learned about myself?

JUSTIFICATION

Many of us became masters at rationalizing what we did. We did it to the point where we refused to accept what others did even when their actions were the same as our own. Even though we cannot force our alcoholic loved ones to change their behavior, we can take a look at our part in the relationship. We can try to see where our actions contributed to the problems. Did we think we were always right, no matter what we did?

Some of us thought everything was the alcoholic's fault, while the rest of us believed we were to blame. Unkindness to anyone for any reason says more about us than it does about the other person. It's not okay to complain, gossip, manipulate, or retaliate in inappropriate ways just because of difficult circumstances. To make progress in recovery, it helps to be objective about our situation and to see our part in it. When we take responsibility for our part, we become willing to try new responses to old problems.

Step Four can help us identify areas where we have tried to justify and rationalize our way through the family disease of alcoholism. It shows us that people who are hurting sometimes hurt other people. As we admit to our own pretenses, we can increase our awareness and improve our personal honesty. In the process, we begin to investigate alternatives.

Reflections

"When we looked closely at ourselves and recalled what we were apt to say and do in various situations, we discovered that our behavior was often distorted by anger, frustration, and fear. That is why many of us reacted to the alcoholic in irrational, hysterical ways. In other words, our actions had not been sane. It would have been only natural for us to think of self-justifying ways to defend what we did, but we learned that our actions were indefensible." (*Al-Anon's Twelve Steps & Twelve Traditions*, p. 14)

Questions

1. My Behavior

What behaviors do I find unacceptable?

What behaviors do I find irritating?

How have I justified my unacceptable actions?

2. Questionable Behavior

How do I feel when I justify my actions with others?

Are there any particular people with whom I consistently engage in unacceptable behavior? Make a list of these people and explain.

Why do I feel it's okay to act out with some and not with others?

How do I behave in ways I would not tolerate from others? What makes me think it is okay for me to act this way?

3. Responses to Unkindness

When someone treats me unkindly, how do I respond? How do I feel about my response?

What would be considered acceptable responses to another's unkindness? List at least three.

Findings

By answering these questions on the subject of justification, what have I learned about myself?

CONTROL

In Al-Anon we hear, "We didn't cause it. We can't control it and we can't cure it." For many of us, our attempts to control the disease of alcoholism brought us into the program. Not only did we try to get the alcoholic to quit drinking, but many of us found our desire to control the alcoholic spilled into other areas of our lives. We insisted that things go as we dictated and we had a difficult time when they did not. We felt that others were trying to sabotage us, when all they were really doing was making choices that were different from ours.

In Al-Anon we learn that the only behavior we have a real chance to control is our own, and that the alcoholic needs to be free to choose as he or she wishes. Keeping the focus on ourselves brings us a new freedom.

Reflections

"One of the effects of alcoholism has been that I have been overly involved in other people's choices. If I feel responsible for someone else's behavior, then I have not detached from whatever I am allowing to embarrass, frustrate, or otherwise bother me. I am still thinking of that person as belonging to me, as a possession rather than an individual. I used to lay out my loved one's clothes, so that his appearance would represent me well. In Al-Anon I learned that by doing this I am really insinuating that he is less able to select what he wishes to wear than I." (. . . *In All Our Affairs*, p. 101)

Questions

1. Family Control

Who was in charge in my home when I was growing up?

How did those in charge control me and was that control helpful or harmful?

Who exercises control in my home now? How?

Who are the important people in my life today and what aspects of their lives do I try to control?

2. Attempting Control

How do I try to control the emotional, financial, and physical lives of my loved ones?

What are some things I do for others that they could do for themselves?

3. Expressing Control

How do I respond when things do not go as I would like them to go?

How do I respond when the people in my life behave in a way I believe is harmful to them?

How do I use other people to try to get what I want?

How do I respond when someone tries to control me?

4. Healthy Interactions

In what ways am I willing to be more flexible in relationships?

How do I show patience when I want someone to hurry up and do things my way?

In what ways do I offer acceptance and understanding during tense moments?

Findings

By answering these questions on the subject of control, what have I learned about myself?

ATTITUDES

Our attitudes are the ways we look at things. Is the glass half empty or half full? Our actions and reactions reveal how the world looks to us. Are we nervous, scared, friendly, or are we ready to fight?

In Al-Anon we hear, "Changed attitudes can aid recovery." All it takes is the willingness to consider viewing our world in a different way. Through a searching and fearless moral inventory, we learn about our personal opinions and how circumstances may have conditioned us to feel, think, and act in certain ways. Little by little we realize that some of our attitudes no longer work.

Our attitudes may have nothing to do with the situation before us. If, for example, our family was unreliable, we may expect everyone to act in that same fashion. We may even react in advance and isolate because we are certain we cannot count on other human beings for help. Such an attitude can hinder progress.

Step One told us we were powerless over alcoholism and the alcoholic, but we do have power over our own attitudes. We have the power to maintain our serenity regardless of the situation at hand. As our Suggested Al-Anon/Alateen Welcome states, "It is possible for us to find contentment, and even happiness, whether the alcoholic is still drinking or not."

God's gifts are all around us. Recognizing and acknowledging them automatically gives us an attitude of gratitude that can work in our favor.

Reflections

"Living with an alcoholic distorted my thinking in many ways, but particularly in one: I blamed all my problems on The Bottle. Now I am learning in Al-Anon to look squarely at each difficulty, not seeking whom to 'blame' but to discover how my attitude helped to create my problem or aggravate it." (*One Day at a Time*, p. 78)

Questions

1. Habits and Feelings

Do I tend to see my cup as half full or half empty? Explain.

What healthy attitudes did I learn from my family?

What poor attitudes did I learn in my family when I was growing up?

How does my attitude change when I am with different people?

2. Behavior Models

What positive characteristics did I admire and consider as role models when I was young? Why?

Which negative characteristics did I reject and avoid when I was young?

How do I feel about people who make more money than I do?

How do I feel about people whose lives are more difficult than mine?

3. Choices

How has knowledge of the disease of alcoholism changed how I perceive the alcoholic(s) in my life?

What happens to my attitude when I focus on the alcoholic?

What happens when I focus on myself rather than on the alcoholic?

What kinds of attitudes do I enjoy in my friends?

Findings

By answering these questions on the subject of attitudes, what have I learned about myself?

COMMUNICATION

In Al-Anon we learn to be more responsible for what we say and do. Initially our communications were based on what we thought the other person wanted to hear, rather than on the facts. Some of us were unable to disagree without shouting, and others found it difficult to express ourselves clearly because we didn't know how we actually felt.

We may have expected our loved ones to read our minds and to anticipate our needs. When they fell short, we became frustrated and angry. Later we began to see that each person in a conversation, including ourselves, is personally accountable.

Having lived with alcoholism, we may have experienced difficulty in speaking up for ourselves or in addressing controversies directly. Al-Anon principles affirm that we are worth it and that we can't hope to have our needs met unless we make those needs known.

We may have found that we didn't have a clue how to really listen to what another person had to say. Our personal agenda has been the only agenda, but Al-Anon encourages us to learn how to be clear and kind in our communications.

Reflections

"Today, by being aware of the words I use, I am learning to communicate more responsibly. I not only share in a more straightforward manner, but I also argue in a healthier way. There are better ways to express myself than to say, 'You did such and such to me.' I can talk about myself and my feelings. I can explain the way I experienced something rather than telling the other person how he or she *made me* feel. I can talk about what I want. I am no longer a victim." (*Courage to Change*, p. 174)

Questions

1. Communication Challenges

Why is it difficult for me to talk to some people and not to others?

What are some of the nonverbal ways that I communicate?

Sometimes my tone of voice interferes with clear communication. What are some examples?

2. Communication Skills

How do I communicate my needs to various people in my life?

What are some of the subjects I am afraid of or that I feel uncomfortable discussing? Why?

What are some examples of both truthful and untruthful statements I have made to others?

How do I communicate with people I do not like?

When was the last time I was in a situation where another person believed that I was entirely wrong? What happened?

3. Understanding Communication

How do I know when someone understands what I have said?

How do I react when someone misunderstands me?

How do I know when I understand what someone says to me?

How do I present myself when I feel strongly about something?

After listening completely to all that was said, what questions do I ask to aid my total understanding?

4. Changing Communication

What did I do in Steps Two and Three that helped me open communication lines between my Higher Power and myself?

How does my attitude toward others affect my communication with them?

Findings

By answering these questions on the subject of communication, what have I learned about myself?

RESPONSIBILITIES

Some of us who lived with active alcoholism confused our responsibilities to others with a feeling that we were responsible for everyone and everything. Though we meant well, our actions may have been intrusive and inappropriate. This resulted in distorted relationships with family and friends.

Others have gone in the opposite direction and become irresponsible. We may have been so consumed with the alcoholic's activities that we couldn't pay attention to our jobs or our children. We may have given up and abandoned our obligations because we believed our efforts didn't matter.

By looking honestly at our responsibilities, we can open the door to improving our relationships.

Reflections

"By process of elimination, I discovered what I am not powerless over—myself. I am responsible for me. I am not responsible for another person's happiness, nor are they responsible for mine." (*Paths to Recovery*, p. 13)

Questions

1. Becoming Responsible

What does my history reveal about me being responsible or irresponsible?

While growing up, what did I learn about being responsible?

What am I teaching others about being responsible?

2. Letting Go of Responsibilities

How do I determine what is my obligation and what is not?

In what ways am I responsible for my family?

How am I responsible for my own happiness?

3. Being Responsible

In what ways am I accountable for my recovery program?

How do I participate in my community through volunteer work, voting, city government, and neighborhood activities?

If I am a parent, how am I involved in my children's schooling?

How do I conduct myself at my job?

4. My Responsibilities Today

Who and what am I responsible for today?

How have I acted responsibly today?

How have I assumed someone else's responsibilities today?

Findings

By answering these questions on the subject of responsibilities, what have I learned about myself?

FINANCES

Alcoholism is an expensive illness. For many people, it took money meant for paying bills and buying family necessities. Over the years, many of us developed a habit of living on leftovers. Even when the family entered recovery, a poverty mentality followed us. We lived in fear of bankruptcy or starvation, long after any emergency had passed.

Even those who have always had unlimited resources regretted wasting money by rescuing loved ones from the consequences of their actions. Some of us denied the truth about each individual situation and continued to spend saying, "This time will be different." Either way, we hoped some miracle would change our circumstances for the better. When the miracle didn't happen, we became resentful.

Fear of financial ruin or the confusion that comes from wasting money may lead us to spend all of our time in a real or imagined survival mode. As a result, other important things can be forgotten. In Al-Anon we learn that with finances, as with all aspects of our lives, it is wise to take care of ourselves, to be responsible, and to practice balance.

For most of us, handling our financial obligations in a responsible way feels very rewarding. By realizing where we came from, asking for help, making new choices, and watching the results, we have worked our way into a better life.

Reflections

> "My financial difficulties were quite real, and my fear and sense of loss were staggering. The stress was terrible. I was again affected by the disease of another, and I owed it to myself to pay attention to my needs and take extra special care of myself. But for the first time, I was able to recognize that my husband was suffering as well and needed my support and my strength. I finally understood what I had so often heard in Al-Anon meetings—that I didn't have to neglect myself in order to care about him." (*How Al-Anon Works*, p. 348)

Questions

1. Managing Money

Who is responsible for the money management in my home?

How much of my monthly expenses are for necessities and how much are for luxuries?

What am I doing to help take care of my future financial needs?

How do I communicate with others about financial responsibilities?

2. My Financial Priorities

What is my credit history?

How do I personally decide about a special purchase?

What have I purchased that was not affordable at the time?

3. Being Financially Responsible

Who provides my financial security?

How am I prepared to earn my own money if the need arises?

Who has met my financial obligations in the past?

What are the ways that I allow financial concerns to take priority over my personal needs?

What role does my Higher Power play in my sense of well-being?

4. Financial Control

How have I used money to try to change someone else's behavior?

When did I inappropriately withhold my financial support?

Findings

By answering these questions on the subject of finances, what have I learned about myself?

GUILT

Some of us believed we were responsible for the alcoholic's unhappiness. We felt as though we had done something wrong. Somehow we thought we caused the drinking and felt guilty about our inability to stop it. A few of us may have thought we could straighten things out if we just tried harder. Convinced that we could make him or her sober and happy, we continued to try to make a difference—even when we thought our mistakes had caused the problem in the first place.

The truth is, everyone makes mistakes and does things wrong. None of us is perfect. It helps to recognize where we might want to change our thinking. It is not appropriate to claim responsibility for the choices of another adult human being. We need only be responsible for our own choices. As one member said, "The alcoholic thought his drinking was my fault, but he was misinformed."

Reflections

"Perhaps the most severe damage to those of us who have shared some part of life with an alcoholic comes in the form of the nagging belief that we are somehow at fault. We may feel it was something we did or did not do—that we were not good enough, not attractive enough, or not clever enough to have solved this problem for the one we love. These are our feelings of guilt." (*Understanding Ourselves and Alcoholism*, p. 4)

Questions

1. Feeling Guilty

Who are the people in my life I feel guilty about?

When did I accept blame for something that was actually not my fault?

How do I treat those I feel guilty about?

What can I do to distinguish between what is my fault and what is not?

2. Making Mistakes

What mistakes have I made at work that I feel guilty about?

How have I wronged my children or my spouse?

What old behaviors of mine pushed me beyond guilt and into feelings of shame?

How responsible am I for the chaos between another person and myself?

3. Making Choices

When something was really my fault and I felt guilty, how did I deal with my feelings?

How has my tendency to feel guilty caused injury to another?

Findings

By answering these questions on the subject of guilt, what have I learned about myself?

SHAME

Alcoholics, unable to cope with their illness, sometimes heaped shame on family members. And we, the loved ones, feared the drinking might indeed be our fault and accepted the shame. Some of us actually came to think of ourselves as mistakes. We may have contributed to the problem drinking through actions that we regret, but we are not responsible for a disease.

Even though we are not guilty, sorting out what is our responsibility and what is not becomes difficult. We might tend to accept responsibility for someone else's mistakes as a way to keep the peace. We may even feel we have harmed everyone with whom we've ever come in contact and forget that we are only human.

Shame is a powerful feeling and involves a loss of self-respect. It may tell us that there is something fundamentally wrong with us, that we never do anything right, or that we are worthless. Shame doesn't allow us the room we need to learn from our errors. Worse yet, our shame becomes a deadly secret.

Reflections

"The greatest obstacle to this learning process is shame. Shame is an excuse to hate ourselves today for something we did or didn't do in the past. There is no room in a shame-filled mind for the fact that we did our best at the time, no room to accept that as human beings we are bound to make mistakes." (*Courage to Change*, p. 57)

Questions

1. My Feelings of Shame

What shameful feelings made it difficult for me to seek help?

What shame do I carry from my past that affects my actions today?

2. Recognizing Shame

When has shame become a defensive crutch for me?

Do I allow my feelings of shame to interfere with my recovery?

3. Choices

How do I treat those individuals I'm ashamed of?

When am I prompted to inflict or to accept shame?

Findings

By answering these questions on the subject of shame, what have I learned about myself?

RELATIONSHIPS

There are many different kinds of relationships and many have multiple levels of intensity. Having been affected by alcoholism, many of us find it difficult to form and sustain close relationships. Our actions often teach people how to treat us. It may be all too obvious that we expect too much or too little from life. We may not know how to interact with people. We may decide that having others in our lives is just not worth the effort, so we deprive ourselves of companionship.

Sometimes the hardest relationships are the ones we didn't choose. These are relationships with family members.

If we're lucky, we eventually learn that both individuals must make an effort in order for a relationship to work, and such work can begin with us. Our behavior can be a powerful example to those around us. As our self-esteem improves, we may enjoy improvements in the quality of our relationships. As we do our best in all of our encounters, people notice and may respond accordingly.

Reflections

"Most of us find that after a while we begin to attract what we give out. If we are consistently warm and respectful, we tend to attract respect and warmth from others." (*How Al-Anon Works*, p. 99)

Questions

1. My Significant Relationships

How do I interact with people in my home, on my job, and in my neighborhood?

Who sets the boundaries in my relationships?

In my interactions with others, what might be harmful about my responses?

How am I honest/dishonest in my relationships?

2. My Role in Relationships

How do I choose my relationships?

What are three positive things I bring to relationships?

What negative behavior am I responsible for in close associations?

What is the difference between "right and wrong" and "their way and my way"?

3. Broken Relationships

What were the main reasons why major relationships in my life ended?

How am I responsible for the chaos in some of my relationships?

How much do I try to control the thinking and actions of others?

4. Relationship Conflicts

How do I treat those with whom I am in conflict?

How do I show respect and tolerance to people in my life?

How do I show others I care for them when I disagree with what they say and do?

Findings

By answering these questions on the subject of relationships, what have I learned about myself?

RUST

By working Al-Anon's Twelve Steps, we learn how to trust a Higher Power, ourselves, and other people. Just how fast we learn to trust depends on our ability to relinquish control, a control we actually did not have in the first place.

In chaotic situations, we learn to trust a Power greater than ourselves to take care of us and our loved ones, whether they are drinking or not. We trust that there is always hope. Eventually we learn to trust our own instincts and our new way of thinking.

As our behaviors and attitudes change, we may meet resistance. It can be difficult to trust ourselves. In Al-Anon we are learning not only to trust our Higher Power, ourselves, and our fellow members, but also that we deserve to be trusted. At first those around us may be doubtful of our new attitudes, but we can earn their trust as well.

Reflections

"When the meeting ended, I would immediately run out without hugging or talking to anyone. No one pushed or chased me down, but they loved me wherever I was and made me feel welcome. Slowly I began to trust, but I never used the phone list or went out with the group for coffee afterwards. Still they loved me. Now and then someone would gently offer a phone number and say, 'Call me if you want to.'

"After several years, I can honestly say I made some of the closest friends of my life. I learned about trust, risks, and reaching out. I'm so grateful for the patience of that group. Al-Anon saved my life and gave me a new one." (The Forum, December 1999, p. 4)

Questions

1. Trusting Myself

What is my history of trusting myself?

In what ways am I trustworthy both to myself and to others?

In what ways have I been untrustworthy in some of my activities?

2. Trusting Other People

How do I determine if someone is trustworthy?

How do I determine if someone has lost my trust?

What behaviors do I have that inspire trust?

What behaviors do I have that inhibit trust?

3. Trusting My Higher Power

What important things do I trust to my Higher Power?

What am I reluctant to give over to my Higher Power at this time?

Findings

By answering these questions on the subject of trust, what have I learned about myself?

COMMITMENT

Because alcoholism is unpredictable, many of us have had difficulty making a decision and sticking to it. A habit of last minute decisions, brought on by our reaction to the drinking, led some of us to become unreliable. After making big plans or taking on too much, we didn't think clearly about how we would follow through. As a result, we became overwhelmed.

As we tried to manipulate our schedules and responsibilities, some of us lost our integrity entirely. We may have been inconsistent in our convictions and positions, so people couldn't count on us. We didn't let those around us know where we stood. We may have vacillated so much, depending on individual situations, that we didn't know where we stood ourselves.

We may also have had a hard time committing to our own recovery and thought our lives were too busy to attend meetings or to get involved in service work. In Al-Anon we learn to take care of ourselves first. We learn to make commitments one day at a time.

Reflections

"When my relationship with a sober alcoholic became unbearable, I tried Al-Anon. Though I felt a degree of peace after my first meeting, I had difficulty making a commitment to anything. When I shared my concern with an Al-Anon member, he told me to just keep coming back. I'm so glad I did, for wonderful changes have happened in my life simply through regular attendance at meetings." (*From Survival to Recovery*, p. 82)

Questions

1. Prioritizing My Commitments

How does my schedule include quiet time, time for meetings, family, and other things I like to do?

How do I determine what I can fit into my schedule?

What portion of my time am I devoting to working on myself?

What are the specific commitments I have in my life today?

2. Being Reliable

How do I follow through on commitments I make?

If I have to break a commitment, how do I do it?

What are some examples of how I keep or don't keep my word?

In what ways does my family count on me to follow through with what I say I will do?

How reliable and prompt am I?

3. My Commitments to Others

What circumstances and/or persons did I consider in the most recent important decisions in my life?

How is my attendance at work or school?

4. My Commitment to Recovery

What is my commitment to attending Al-Anon meetings?

When the time comes, what will most likely be my reasons for being or not being available as a Sponsor to those who ask?

What am I willing to commit to in Al-Anon in order to give back to others what I can?

Findings

By answering these questions on the subject of commitment, what have I learned about myself?

When we first come to Al-Anon, many of us are overwhelmed by self-pity. We may be so frustrated by our living situation that we cannot see anything positive. We think we never have any good luck. The alcoholic's illness and our reactions to it may overshadow anything pleasant. It's as if the sun is out, but all we see are clouds.

When faced with challenges, Al-Anon suggests that we pay attention to the good things in our lives. Gratitude can be a powerful antidote to despair and hopelessness. By being thankful, we learn it is within our power to maintain our serenity and to have a good day, regardless of what choices our loved ones are making.

Reflections

"The self-pity that I have been comfortable with for so long needs to be replaced with gratitude. Sure, there are plenty of reasons that I could cry, 'Poor Me,' but I have a much longer list of things to be thankful for. I am learning to thank God each morning for His gift: a beautiful day, no matter what the weather or the problems." (*. . . In All Our Affairs*, p. 232)

Questions

1. Gifts from My Higher Power

What are three things I could have been grateful for the last time someone treated me unkindly or unfairly?

What are the top ten things that I am always grateful for?

What are five daily things I am grateful for that are different from my top ten?

What would I list if I were to write the alphabet and think of one thing, beginning with each letter, for which I am grateful?

2. Opportunities for Gratitude

What can I be grateful for when people make me angry?

Besides earning a living, what other reasons do I have for liking my job?

3. Expressing My Gratitude

How do my actions show my gratitude?

What changes am I grateful for that have come about because of the Al-Anon program?

Findings

By answering these questions on the subject of gratitude, what have I learned about myself?

LOVE

After years of living in the grasp of the disease of alcoholism, it may be difficult for us to love other people, and loving ourselves may seem like a foreign concept. Making another person our top priority may have robbed us and them of dignity or respect. Some of us may have felt that we didn't deserve to be loved.

For the first time, many of us tried to learn how to show our love for the alcoholic without supporting his or her destructive actions. We knew it was possible because we saw others in the Al-Anon program respond to the same situations with love and respect. Eventually we have come to believe that love is one of the best recovery tools available.

Reflections

"I needed love before I even knew what it was. Now that I understand something about it, I need it even more. By loving myself, I not only take care of my own needs, but I lay a foundation for loving others. By loving others, I learn to treat myself well." (*Courage to Change*, p. 42)

Questions

1. Loving Myself

What do I love about myself?

What are things I like and dislike about my actions?

How do I express love for myself?

2. Expressing My Love

How do I show love for my Higher Power?

What are some examples of how I express my love for others?

How do I show compassion for those I love?

Besides people, what else do I love?

3. Loving the Person, Not the Disease

How have my expectations of those I love/loved caused problems for me?

What are five ways I have acted lovingly toward others?

How have I been unkind toward someone who is important to me?

4. Loving Relationships

How is it difficult or not difficult for me to fall in love?

How do I know that I am capable of loving another person?

What can I do today that will show my love for others and for myself?

Findings

By answering these questions on the subject of love, what have I learned about myself?

INTIMACY

When we come to Al-Anon, many of us have lived in isolation. Worried about what others would think, we lived our lives cautiously, afraid to let anyone know what was really going on inside. We may even have shut out our family and close friends. Some of us were reluctant to interact with new people and had few, if any, close relationships. As a result, we may have been lonely and felt that no one understood.

In Al-Anon we find many of these experiences are common to others in the program. Eventually we see that the friends we make in Al-Anon can become our confidants and strong supporters. By sharing in meetings, we start to trust others, to reason things out without gossip, and to earn mutual respect.

Intimate relationships can help us grow. As we become more open with those in our lives, we find we can rely on them to encourage us and to give us honest feedback. Eventually we use what we learn to strengthen our relationships with family members and friends.

Reflections

"My biggest complaint was my husband's lack of support. I looked to him for companionship, for conversation, caring about my troubles, sharing my religion, and on and on.

"It came to me slowly but surely that I did have this relationship in my life—with Al-Anon friends. My spiritual journey was being taken with my Sponsor; another Al-Anon friend was willing to listen to my job-related problems and give me input; another shared my grief and my journey to peace when my beloved sister died; I had but to make a phone call and someone would join me for a cup of coffee or a walk in our beautiful nature preserve nearby. I had it all—in different people, but all loving and caring for me. This realization led me to peace, gratitude, and letting go of the demands on my husband to be 'everything' for me." (*. . . In All Our Affairs*, p. 231)

Questions

1. Being Intimate

How do I define intimacy?

What actions encourage intimacy and which ones don't?

Which of my actions are helpful in bringing me closer to another person?

2. Learning about Intimacy

With whom was I intimate when I was growing up?

How have I shared important information with someone I didn't trust?

Where do I get examples of positive, intimate relationships?

3. Expressing Intimacy

In what ways have I been intellectually or spiritually intimate with the alcoholic?

What activities help me show how much certain people mean to me?

What kind of examples do my actions convey about the value of close relationships?

Findings

By answering these questions on the subject of intimacy, what have I learned about myself?

MATURITY

Somewhere along the way many of us affected by alcoholism stopped growing emotionally. Consequently in some areas of our lives we can be adults who have the reactions of children. It is possible that we do not know how to conduct ourselves in an appropriate manner simply because we never learned how.

Maturity means acting our age. We are being mature when we have a realistic view of our situation. We let those around us live their lives and we elect to accept responsibility for ourselves. We also stop criticizing or expressing our rage and begin to weigh our thoughts and emotions. When we are mature, we speak up for ourselves and are kind to others. We display good balance and we conduct ourselves with calm confidence.

Mature people are not perfect and they know it, but most are willing to look at themselves honestly with the intention of continuing to learn and grow. It is always possible to call on our Higher Power to help us see where we can be more mature.

Reflections

"A big step toward maturing is to realize that I cannot change conditions by running away from them. I can only change my point of view about them and their relation to me—and this can be done only by changing myself." (*One Day at a Time*, p. 214)

Questions

1. Mature Considerations

How do I react when someone makes a demand of me?

How do I use what I hear from others to help me deal with situations?

What do I do when someone asks me a question and I don't know the answer?

2. Maturity in My Relationships

How do I react to people who offer me suggestions?

How do I respond when someone tells me I have made a mistake?

What do I do when someone asks me a question that I don't want to answer?

How do I try to get my way in an argument?

3. Choices

What are five things I do in arguments and/or discussions that affect the way I feel?

Why do I get involved in disagreements?

4. Mature Responsibilities

Can I be open to another person's opinion?

How do I form and strengthen my own opinions?

What is my responsibility while discussing an issue with someone who has an opinion that is different from mine?

Findings

By answering these questions on the subject of maturity, what have I learned about myself?

SEX

When two people in a relationship share feelings of attraction, hope, and an opportunity for closeness, it is possible for their sexuality to blossom. Sharing sexual pleasure can take the relationship a step further and create a special bond. The quality and longevity of such a bond may depend on many characteristics in both individuals.

Closeness with someone who has been affected by alcoholism can be a challenge, as he or she may become emotionally unavailable or physically unable to respond. Even without any active drinking involved, some of us may find the idea of sex with our loved one difficult or at least awkward. For many reasons, we may also find ourselves unable to participate in the relationship physically or emotionally.

Some of us have used sex as a way to feel needed and loved, while others even refused to consider it an option. Some of us used sex as a bargaining chip to get what we wanted. We may have accepted sex as a reward for putting up with unacceptable behavior. We may have felt intoxicated by the illusion of intimacy and the temporary gratification that we experienced physically, emotionally, or both.

Infidelity can be a problem for either partner in a relationship. Past experiences of abuse or abandonment can provoke powerful reactions that may be destructive to a current relationship. Especially in alcoholic relationships, some of us have looked elsewhere because we believed someone might be more understanding, or at least make us feel better for a moment.

Because sexual involvement offers the possibility of great rewards as well as dangers, it is certainly worth our time to see what we think and how we feel about sex.

Reflections

"We were both self-conscious about sex after sobriety, [and] we spoiled what might have been a wonderful closeness. I think there were leftovers from my childhood days, too. I disliked my father for his drunken demands and I carried that feeling into all my relationships. I had to take an inventory with professional help." (*Living with Sobriety*, p. 40)

Questions

1. Expressing My Sexuality

What do I share with my significant other that shows him/her how I feel?

How do I feel about discussing sex with my partner?

How have I discussed my sexual needs with my partner?

How do I say no when I prefer not to have sex?

How have I used sex to control my partner?

What is my definition of faithfulness?

How have I been unfaithful in a relationship?

2. Sexual Boundaries

What are my requirements for engaging in sexual activity?

How do I determine when it's okay to engage in sexual intimacy with my partner?

3. Special Concerns

How satisfied am I with my current level of sexual activity?

What areas of my sexual behavior am I responsible for?

Who initiates sex between my loved one and myself?

Are there any other issues about sex that are bothering me?

Findings

By answering these questions on the subject of sexuality, what have I learned about myself?

VALUES

Values encompass our personal beliefs about the right way to live. Some of us decide how to behave and interact with others based on what we feel is morally right. When we first come to Al-Anon, many of us feel confused about what our values really are.

Some of us have spent so much time and energy coping with alcoholism that we aren't sure what we believe. We may have pushed our values aside in order to keep peace in our alcoholic home. We might have even ignored what we believe is right and acted contrary to our beliefs. For example, if we feel it is morally wrong to cheat on our income taxes, we might still have signed an inaccurate joint return, if the alcoholic insisted, to avoid conflict. Perhaps we found a joke offensive but we didn't speak up, fearful of looking like we didn't belong with the crowd.

In Al-Anon we are learning what our principles truly are, and how to practice them in all of our thoughts and actions. Acting with integrity based upon our own value system can be an important way to take care of ourselves.

Reflections

"In my Fourth Step, I discovered that I had values that I had chosen to ignore or deny in order to please others or because it seemed the 'easy' way. I learned not to worry so much about what others thought of me, but to pay attention to what I thought was right." (. . . *In All Our Affairs*, p. 45)

Questions

1. Personal Standards

What are my values and how did I form them?

How do the values of my childhood differ from the values I have today?

When do I remain true to my values, or make exceptions to them?

What were some of the circumstances when I went against my value system? Were there consequences?

2. Expressing My Values

How do I treat individuals whose values are different from my own?

What happens when my values clash with someone else's?

Findings

By answering these questions on the subject of values, what have I learned about myself?

CHARACTER TRAITS

It has been said that all of us have three characters: Who we think we are, who we want others to believe we are, and who we really are. In fact we are combinations of all three. Our moral and ethical strengths are traits that were forged from the formative years of childhood into the shapes of the present. Whether they are set firmly now depends on our thinking, what others think of us, and the reality of our natures.

The quality of our character is dependent on the many traits that contribute to our thinking and our behavior. When we examine the parts that make up the whole, we are more likely to see just where our strengths and weaknesses lie. We can see in what way certain qualities express themselves. In this way we can gain insight into the "exact nature of our wrongs" and help ourselves to find a direction for improving our shortcomings.

Reflections

"Some of my good qualities are: I'm smart, I'm a good listener, I'm understanding, independent, responsible and funny. I'm also likable, caring, supportive, sensitive, trustworthy, and reliable.

"When someone criticizes me, first I start to wonder why they're picking on me. Then I usually stop, listen, and learn.

"It was hard to accept myself, though, at first. I thought I was the worst person I knew and that no one would like me for myself. Then I went away on an Alateen weekend event and did my Fourth Step inventory. I got to know myself and, at first, I didn't like myself very much. The whole idea of the Fourth Step and self-acceptance was so new to me. But gradually I began to learn about myself, and the most amazing thing happened—I started to love me." (*Courage to Be Me*, p. 122)

Questions

Although we tend to lean toward one trait or another, we will probably find that we fluctuate between the extremes listed in the questions below. Of course, our goal is progress not perfection.

Aware of others **Self-centered**

Do I try to become less preoccupied with myself by getting interested in things outside myself?

Can I see that being helpful to others is a way out of my dilemma?

Are my responsibilities to myself kept in good balance with my desire to reach out to others?

Helpful to others **Self-indulgent**

Do I enjoy going out of my way for others, or am I constantly expecting others to go out of their way for me?

Have I considered helping out at my Al-Anon group by accepting a responsibility?

Generous **Selfish**

Do I make an effort to consider the needs of others as well as my own?

Am I generous with my time in service to others, especially my family members?

Do I try to share something of myself, such as my feelings and ideas, with others?

Thoughtful **Self-pitying**

Have I considered that others may have had as difficult a time in life as I have?

Do I steer clear of getting others to feel sorry for me?

Do I see problems as one of the greatest forces for growth in my life, a real gift from my Higher Power?

Open-minded, gracious **Smug, stubborn**

Can I be open-minded and receptive to people who have new ideas?

Can I compromise realistically?

Can I do things the way another person suggests?

Perceptive **Judgmental**

Do I avoid taking another person's inventory?

When I am speaking about other people, have I eliminated words from my vocabulary that claim what they *should do* and what they *ought to do*?

Am I convinced that most people are the way they feel they need to be at present, not necessarily the way they would like to be?

Respectful **Disrespectful**

Do I respect the feelings and experiences of others?

Have I developed some sense of my right to be treated with dignity?

Can I balance my need to fulfill myself as a person with knowledge of the same needs that other people have?

Patient **Impatient**

Do I have patience with myself while maintaining a healthy form of self-discipline?

Can I patiently teach others what I have learned and appreciate their willingness to learn?

Do I realize that in being patient I am giving my Higher Power the time to give me the guidance that I need?

Tolerant **Intolerant**

Can I accommodate people and situations and still maintain my self-respect?

Do I avoid condescending attitudes toward others?

Do I realize that my feelings of frustration decrease as my tolerance increases?

Realistic **Unrealistic**

Do I understand that reality is what is happening, not what I *think* or *feel* is happening?

Can I see that facing the truth by itself means not having to deal with dozens of imagined troubles?

Do I believe what is real happens only one day at a time?

Reasonable **Unreasonable**

Do I try to reason things out rather than act on impulse?

Do I try to hear a full story before drawing my conclusions?

Can I give others the benefit of the doubt?

Assertive **Submissive**

Do I act on my own behalf and set my own goals?

Do I make my own decisions?

Can I resist giving in just to keep peace when my own welfare and integrity are involved?

Cooperative **Domineering**

Do I try to understand another person's position, even though I may not agree with it?

Can I work well with others in a group?

Can I accept the leadership of others?

Do I lead by example as well as by words?

Outgoing **Withdrawn**

Am I comfortable in my social interactions with others?

Do I realize that others may benefit from my experience if I share it?

Do I involve myself in the affairs of the world, my community, and my family?

Forgiving **Resentful**

Do I see making a list of resentments as a first step toward rooting them out?

Once a conflict is over and I have expressed my anger, can I let it go?

Can I offer understanding if involvement in AA occupies a good deal of the alcoholic's time?

Trusting **Suspicious**

Can I give others the benefit of the doubt?

Can I risk disappointment in order to invest in a new relationship?

Do I avoid constantly searching for hidden motives behind what other people say or do?

Trustworthy **Prone to gossip**

Do I avoid discussing another's problems under the guise of it being "for their own good"?

Do I avoid tattling on others?

Do I see protecting confidences as an essential part of the Al-Anon program and as a hallmark of a mature person?

Content **Envious**

Do I make a conscious effort to count my blessings?

Can I enjoy the good fortune of others?

Can I avoid blaming others and try to improve my own circumstances?

Agreeable **Disagreeable**

Do I look for the best in each person and situation that I encounter?

Do I avoid arguing simply for the sake of arguing?

Do I avoid the use of sarcasm when others do not share my views?

Cheerful **Depressed**

Do I avoid blaming others for my unhappiness?

Can I understand why Abraham Lincoln said, "Most folks are as happy as they make up their minds to be"?

Do I recover quickly from disappointment?

Courteous **Discourteous**

Do I listen attentively when others are talking, or am I just waiting for my turn to speak?

Am I considerate of others in my use of language and the tone and pitch of my voice?

Do I know the difference between asking for help and imposing?

Kind **Unkind**

Do I treat others kindly and consider their feelings?

If I find it difficult to be kind, do I try to refrain from saying anything?

Do I see value in simply lending a listening ear to someone in need?

Loving, caring **Indifferent**

Do I avoid an I-don't-care attitude about others, realizing that indifference can be more cruel than outright rejection?

Do I try to avoid being overbearing and overly protective?

Can I accept the love that others offer to me?

Discreet **Lacking discretion**

Am I conscientious and tactful in my interaction with others, always considering their feelings?

Do I avoid talking too much about one point or another?

Have I considered listening to myself as a means of developing a sense of discretion?

Stable **Panicky, violent**

Do I work to avoid wide swings in my moods?

Do I express my feelings in appropriate ways?

Am I sensitive to the feelings of others in a healthy way?

Do I use silence to help me regain stability and composure?

Consistent **Inconsistent**

Do I say what I mean and mean what I say?

Do I do what I have promised to do?

Do I act the same way in similar situations on different occasions?

Sincere **Insincere**

Do I try to be myself and avoid putting on a front to impress others?

Do I mean it when I give a compliment?

Do I avoid manipulating people by telling them what they want to hear instead of what I really think or feel?

Honest **Dishonest**

Am I honest with myself about my motives?

Do I avoid rationalizing or justifying my faults?

Can I keep from telling lies, even small ones?

Can I be straightforward with others, letting them know me as I really am?

Am I careful never to be hostile or vicious under the guise of honesty?

Willing to admit faults **Self-righteous**

Can I admit to myself and other people when I am wrong?

Do I avoid following up an apology with an excuse for my behavior?

Have I grown past the point where I rationalize and claim my bad behavior is reasonable because of my situation?

Humble **Arrogant**

Am I a gracious winner?

Am I aware that being humble is having an honest appraisal of myself?

Do I know that a *humbling* experience is never a *humiliating* one?

Have I learned that humility means having a sense of proportion between me and my Higher Power?

Calm **Worrisome**

Can I listen to other people's problems without worrying about them?

Do I realize that action is often an antidote to worry?

Do I use the Serenity Prayer to find a sense of peace?

Relaxed **Tense**

Is there something I really enjoy doing that will help me relax?

Can I realize that a realistic amount of tension in most situations keeps me alert and helps me to function well?

Can I use the slogan, "Easy Does It," to my advantage?

Confident, having faith **Fearful, apprehensive**

Have I ever listed and analyzed my fears?

Do I see value in talking to someone about my fears?

Can I accept a certain amount of insecurity in my life without fearing that everything will fall apart?

Hopeful **Despondent**

Can I start each day with hopes of making it better than the one before?

Am I willing to do what I can to fulfill my hopes?

Do I believe in a Higher Power who can help me find a better, happier way of life?

Do I try to expect the best in each situation I encounter?

Do I give myself a chance to have a bright future?

Do I try to share the best part of myself in my relationships with others?

Living for today **Living in the past, worrying about the future**

Have I done all I can to rid myself of guilty feelings about the past?

Do I exercise all my senses in positive ways?

Am I willing to apply the "Just for Today" concepts in my life?

Industrious **Lazy**

Do I realize that willingness to do something is the first step toward actually doing it?

Can I stick to a task once I've started it?

Do I have an organized way of tackling my duties?

Prompt **Procrastinating**

Do I try to avoid thoughtless delays in actions or decisions because of my laziness or carelessness?

Do I realize that procrastination often leads to justification for missed opportunities?

Am I aware that being late shows disrespect to those waiting for me?

Purposeful **Aimless**

Do I still care enough to make changes in my life?

Do I have a purpose in my life?

Can I discipline myself in healthy and comfortable ways so that I can accomplish things?

Responsible **Irresponsible**

Can people trust me with responsibility?

Have I learned to say no sometimes?

Do I avoid feeling responsible for others' lives but see myself as having responsibilities to others?

Using talents and abilities **Disinterested in self**

Do I appreciate my talents and abilities?

Can I discipline myself enough to develop my talents and abilities?

Do I realize that my talents are gifts and use them in service to my Higher Power and my fellow man?

Thankful **Ungrateful**

Am I thankful for present blessings?

Have I ever made a list of things I am grateful for?

Do I take time to express my thanks to my Higher Power?

Willing to continue to seek emotional and spiritual balance **Smug, complacent**

Do I know that I have not finished my recovery when I have completed the Fourth Step?

Am I willing to continue working the Steps beyond Step Four?

Findings

After answering these questions on the subject of character traits, what have I learned about myself?

Used in conjunction with the questions in the section entitled "Character Traits," this checklist can give us an idea of where we see ourselves in relation to these traits. Although we tend to lean toward one trait or another, we will probably find that we fluctuate between the extremes listed here. Again, our goal is progress not perfection.

DATE: ______________

Place a checkmark where you see yourself today.

Aware of others	❑	❑	❑	❑	❑	**Self-centered**
Helpful to others	❑	❑	❑	❑	❑	**Self-indulgent**
Generous	❑	❑	❑	❑	❑	**Selfish**
Thoughtful	❑	❑	❑	❑	❑	**Self-pitying**
Open-minded, gracious	❑	❑	❑	❑	❑	**Smug, stubborn**
Perceptive	❑	❑	❑	❑	❑	**Judgmental**
Respectful	❑	❑	❑	❑	❑	**Disrespectful**
Patient	❑	❑	❑	❑	❑	**Impatient**
Tolerant	❑	❑	❑	❑	❑	**Intolerant**
Realistic	❑	❑	❑	❑	❑	**Unrealistic**
Reasonable	❑	❑	❑	❑	❑	**Unreasonable**
Assertive	❑	❑	❑	❑	❑	**Submissive**
Cooperative	❑	❑	❑	❑	❑	**Domineering**
Outgoing	❑	❑	❑	❑	❑	**Withdrawn**
Forgiving	❑	❑	❑	❑	❑	**Resentful**
Trusting	❑	❑	❑	❑	❑	**Suspicious**

Trustworthy	❑	❑	❑	❑	❑	**Prone to gossip**
Content	❑	❑	❑	❑	❑	**Envious**
Agreeable	❑	❑	❑	❑	❑	**Disagreeable**
Cheerful	❑	❑	❑	❑	❑	**Depressed**
Courteous	❑	❑	❑	❑	❑	**Discourteous**
Kind	❑	❑	❑	❑	❑	**Unkind**
Loving, caring	❑	❑	❑	❑	❑	**Indifferent**
Discreet	❑	❑	❑	❑	❑	**Lacking discretion**
Stable	❑	❑	❑	❑	❑	**Panicky, violent**
Consistent	❑	❑	❑	❑	❑	**Inconsistent**
Sincere	❑	❑	❑	❑	❑	**Insincere**
Honest	❑	❑	❑	❑	❑	**Dishonest**
Willing to admit faults	❑	❑	❑	❑	❑	**Self-righteous**
Humble	❑	❑	❑	❑	❑	**Arrogant**
Calm	❑	❑	❑	❑	❑	**Worrisome**
Relaxed	❑	❑	❑	❑	❑	**Tense**
Confident, having faith	❑	❑	❑	❑	❑	**Fearful, apprehensive**
Hopeful	❑	❑	❑	❑	❑	**Despondent**
Living for today	❑	❑	❑	❑	❑	**Living in the past, worrying about the future**
Industrious	❑	❑	❑	❑	❑	**Lazy**

Prompt	❑	❑	❑	❑	❑	**Procrastinating**
Purposeful	❑	❑	❑	❑	❑	**Aimless**
Responsible	❑	❑	❑	❑	❑	**Irresponsible**
Using talents and abilities	❑	❑	❑	❑	❑	**Disinterested in self**
Thankful	❑	❑	❑	❑	❑	**Ungrateful**
Willing to continue to seek emotional and spiritual balance	❑	❑	❑	❑	❑	**Smug, complacent**

Findings

By noting where I am right now on this list of character traits, what have I learned about myself?

SPIRITUALITY

Al-Anon is a spiritual program of recovery. Though we are powerless over the disease of alcoholism, we can rely on a Power greater than ourselves to guide us.

Some of us may have had a relationship with the God of our understanding when we first came to Al-Anon, while others needed to develop that relationship. Even this may have been a leap of faith, since some of us may not have believed in any sort of Power greater than ourselves, or what we did believe in may have had a negative, vengeful, or punishing connotation. Still others held that any Higher Power was far too busy to be concerned with our daily problems.

In Al-Anon we are simply asked to "come to believe" that there is a force at work larger than we are and that we are free to address such a Power however we choose. We can use the same words we used as children, or we can turn to nature, the universe, or our Al-Anon group. We can even think of our Higher Power as "not me."

Al-Anon encourages us to believe that we are not totally in control and to trust that with the help of such a dependable Higher Power, our lives are unfolding exactly as they should.

Reflections

"I came to believe in Al-Anon first and that good feeling that I got when I came into the meeting room. Many weeks went by with me saying the Serenity Prayer and referring to Al-Anon as the Power. People also suggested I think about this Higher Power as fate, nature, or anything that is good. And it started to work. I turned my will and my life over to Al-Anon, fate, and nature." (. . . *In All Our Affairs*, p. 34)

Questions

1. My Spiritual Background

What was my childhood experience of a Higher Power?

How has my concept of God or a Higher Power changed through the years?

What evidence do I have of a Higher Power in my life?

What have I trusted to my Higher Power so far?

2. Expressing My Spirituality

What forms of prayer and meditation do I use to communicate with my Higher Power?

How often do I pray and meditate?

Of the things that concern me the most, which ones do I leave to my Higher Power?

What are the reasons that there are still things I don't trust to my Higher Power?

3. My Spiritual Priorities

What do I consider most important in my life?

What situations in my life do I feel the most joy or the most sadness about?

When do I feel the most calm and serene?

How do I use the Serenity Prayer in my daily life?

What about myself am I embarrassed or ashamed to tell another person or even my Higher Power?

4. My Spiritual Connection

How does my Higher Power work in my daily life?

How does my Higher Power express love to me?

How do I express love and gratitude to my Higher Power?

Findings

By answering these questions on the subject of spirituality, what have I learned about myself?

IN SUMMARY

After writing a searching and fearless moral inventory of ourselves, one thing is clear. We are still here. Hopefully we are here with a better understanding of who we are and why we are this way. At this point our fear of investigation may not be as intense as it once was and we might even feel a little better about ourselves. Now our personal goals for recovery, peace, and serenity are probably easier to define.

Completion of this Fourth Step inventory provides us with tools that can keep us on the road to a more manageable life. Such tools help us find balance, acceptance, and love for ourselves as well as for the other significant people in our lives. Our conclusions drawn from the Fourth Step depend on our individual judgment. The results, along with guidance from our Sponsor, can help us determine the course of our own recovery, despite any adverse circumstances that may develop in our lives.

Questions

1. In my "Findings" for each section of this workbook, what did I learn about myself when I looked at:

Honesty

Self-Worth

Fear

Anger

Resentment

Justification

Control

Attitudes

Communication

Responsibilities

Finances

Guilt

Shame

Relationships

Trust

Commitment

Gratitude

Love

Intimacy

Maturity

Sex

Values

Character Traits

Character Checklist

Spirituality

2. As a result of my searching and fearless moral inventory, how do I feel and what do I think about myself right now?

Suggestions

Those of us who are serious about self-improvement will discover real progress if we periodically review what we have done.

As a matter of privacy and possibly of personal safety, it is helpful to keep this workbook in a safe place. For validation and reference, we can go to our *Blueprint for Progress* workbook the way we would visit a trustworthy Sponsor, friend, or a relative who knows all about us and loves us unconditionally.

Using Step Four and other Al-Anon tools can help us develop our own personalized program of recovery. In so doing, working the program becomes having a life and living life—our own life, not someone else's.

Reflections

"I must go on day after day trying to face myself as I am, and to correct whatever is keeping me from growing into the person I want to be.

"As I review each day and think over the consequences of what I have said and done, I can go on to Step Five . . ." (*One Day at a Time*, p. 171)

TWELVE STEPS

1. We admitted we were powerless over alcohol—that our lives had become unmanageable.
2. Came to believe that a Power greater than ourselves could restore us to sanity.
3. Made a decision to turn our will and our lives over to the care of God *as we understood Him*.
4. Made a searching and fearless moral inventory of ourselves.
5. Admitted to God, to ourselves, and to another human being the exact nature of our wrongs.
6. Were entirely ready to have God remove all these defects of character.
7. Humbly asked Him to remove our shortcomings.
8. Made a list of all persons we had harmed, and became willing to make amends to them all.
9. Made direct amends to such people wherever possible, except when to do so would injure them or others.
10. Continued to take personal inventory and when we were wrong promptly admitted it.
11. Sought through prayer and meditation to improve our conscious contact with God *as we understood Him*, praying only for knowledge of His will for us and the power to carry that out.
12. Having had a spiritual awakening as the result of these steps, we tried to carry this message to others, and to practice these principles in all our affairs.

TWELVE TRADITIONS

1. Our common welfare should come first; personal progress for the greatest number depends upon unity.
2. For our group purpose there is but one authority—a loving God as He may express Himself in our group conscience. Our leaders are but trusted servants—they do not govern.
3. The relatives of alcoholics, when gathered together for mutual aid, may call themselves an Al-Anon Family Group, provided that, as a group, they have no other affiliation. The only requirement for membership is that there be a problem of alcoholism in a relative or friend.
4. Each group should be autonomous, except in matters affecting another group or Al-Anon or AA as a whole.
5. Each Al-Anon Family Group has but one purpose: to help families of alcoholics. We do this by practicing the Twelve Steps of AA *ourselves*, by encouraging and understanding our alcoholic relatives, and by welcoming and giving comfort to families of alcoholics.
6. Our Family Groups ought never endorse, finance or lend our name to any outside enterprise, lest problems of money, property and prestige divert us from our primary spiritual aim. Although a separate entity, we should always co-operate with Alcoholics Anonymous.
7. Every group ought to be fully self-supporting, declining outside contributions.
8. Al-Anon Twelfth Step work should remain forever non-professional, but our service centers may employ special workers.
9. Our groups, as such, ought never be organized; but we may create service boards or committees directly responsible to those they serve.
10. The Al-Anon Family Groups have no opinion on outside issues; hence our name ought never be drawn into public controversy.
11. Our public relations policy is based on attraction rather than promotion; we need always maintain personal anonymity at the level of press, radio, films, and TV. We need guard with special care the anonymity of all AA members.
12. Anonymity is the spiritual foundation of all our Traditions, ever reminding us to place principles above personalities.

TWELVE CONCEPTS OF SERVICE

1. The ultimate responsibility and authority for Al-Anon world services belongs to the Al-Anon groups.
2. The Al-Anon Family Groups have delegated complete administrative and operational authority to their Conference and its service arms.
3. The right of decision makes effective leadership possible.
4. Participation is the key to harmony.
5. The rights of appeal and petition protect minorities and insure that they be heard.
6. The Conference acknowledges the primary administrative responsibility of the Trustees.
7. The Trustees have legal rights while the rights of the Conference are traditional.
8. The Board of Trustees delegates full authority for routine management of Al-Anon Headquarters to its executive committees.
9. Good personal leadership at all service levels is a necessity. In the field of world service the Board of Trustees assumes the primary leadership.
10. Service responsibility is balanced by carefully defined service authority and double-headed management is avoided.
11. The World Service Office is composed of selected committees, executives and staff members.
12. The spiritual foundation for Al-Anon's world services is contained in the General Warranties of the Conference, Article 12 of the Charter.

GENERAL WARRANTIES OF THE CONFERENCE

In all proceedings the World Service Conference of Al-Anon shall observe the spirit of the Traditions:

1. that only sufficient operating funds, including an ample reserve, be its prudent financial principle;
2. that no Conference member shall be placed in unqualified authority over other members;
3. that all decisions be reached by discussion vote and whenever possible by unanimity;
4. that no Conference action ever be personally punitive or an incitement to public controversy;
5. that though the Conference serves Al-Anon it shall never perform any act of government; and that like the fellowship of Al-Anon Family Groups which it serves, it shall always remain democratic in thought and action.

NOTES

NOTES

NOTES